About the Book

Today people all over the world go scuba diving. They use the aqualung, an underwater breathing device, to stay beneath the sea for lengthy periods. This might not be possible if it were not for the inventions and experiments of one Frenchman— Jacques-Yves Cousteau.

Jacques' love of the sea led to the invention of the aqualung. With the aid of this, and special watertight cameras, he later filmed depths never before seen by man. Aboard his research ship, the *Calypso,* he travels the seas exploring and researching the waters of the world. He has studied the shy octopus and the walrus. In the Aegean Sea he hunted for the legendary city of Atlantis. He is director of one of the largest marine museums and laboratories, where scientists from all over the world go to study.

Today the waters have been ravaged by pollution. It is men like Jacques Cousteau who are working to understand, protect, and save the sea.

Jacques Cousteau

by Genie Iverson
illustrations by Hal Ashmead

G.P. Putnam's Sons   New York

For my mother and father

Seven-year-old Jacques-Yves Cousteau floated on his back off-shore. A wave washed over his face. He licked his lips and grinned. They tasted as salty as the sea he loved.

Jacques was born on June 11, 1910, at St.-André-de-Cubzac in France. His family spent summers by the sea, and it was there that he learned to swim.

When Jacques was ten years old, his family visited the United States. They lived in New York City, and Jacques learned to play stickball with the neighborhood children.

During the summer Jacques went to a camp in Vermont. He was warned not to dive into the lake from the pier. A dead tree limb lay deep in the water. If a boy were caught in its branches, he could drown.

Jacques waded out from shore to the end of the pier. He took a deep breath and dove into the muddy water.

He felt along the slimy bottom
until his hands brushed against a
branch.

Jacques was almost out of
breath. He gave one big tug, and
the branch came loose from the

bottom. He pulled it to the surface.

Other boys helped drag the
branch ashore. Now they could
dive safely all summer long.

Home again in France, Jacques discovered that home movie cameras were being sold for the first time. Machines and gadgets fascinated him. Secretly he saved enough money to buy a camera. The first thing he did was take it apart to learn how it worked. He dreamed of a movie company of his own.

On letter paper he printed his
company's name:

But Jacques' moviemaking was interrupted when his father found the camera.

"So this is why your grades have dropped," Monsieur Cousteau said to the thirteen-year-old filmmaker. "You'd better let me keep this until you catch up in school."

Jacques studied harder than ever before. Within a month he had his camera back.

When Jacques was nineteen, he became a cadet at the French Naval Academy at Brest. He sailed around the world aboard a naval training ship.

Soon after being graduated he was in a car accident.

In the hospital, doctors bandaged his broken bones. The nerve in his left arm was dead, they said. "Lieutenant, I think you should get used to the idea that you will have to wear a brace."

"I can't accept that," Jacques said.

Sent to a ship in the Mediterranean to get well, Jacques exercised his left arm. He swam every day in the warm sea. Slowly he won back the use of his arm.

After he recovered completely, a shipmate gave him a pair of watertight goggles. Wading out from the shore, Jacques slipped the goggles over his eyes and dove.

Wide-eyed, he stared at what he saw.

Swaying forests of brown and green seaweed clung to rocks. Tiny silver fish darted through the water. He had discovered a silent new world—the world beneath the surface of the sea.

In 1937 Jacques married Si-
mone Melchior, the daughter of a
French naval officer. She, too,
loved the sea. Later they had two
sons.

In his free time, Cousteau con-
tinued to explore the sea. He
now wore diving fins. He glided
down past grotto walls covered

with sea urchins, lobsters, and starfish. A school of fish darted away from him and disappeared into the shadowy depths below. Cousteau started after them but then turned back. He was almost out of breath.

If only he didn't have to return to the surface for air. If only he could stay down longer to explore.

Maybe he could carry tanks of air on his back. If he invented a machine that would feed him enough air, he could stay underwater like a fish.

Cousteau drew plans for the new machine, but he had to put them away when World War II started. German and Italian soldiers were trying to invade his country. He went to war aboard a French naval cruiser.

In 1940 France fell to its enemies. The French Navy was forced to stop fighting.

Now Cousteau would work on his underwater breathing machine. He hurried to Paris with his plans. There he met Émile Gagnan, an expert in handling gases.

The two men set to work building their invention, which they called the aqualung.

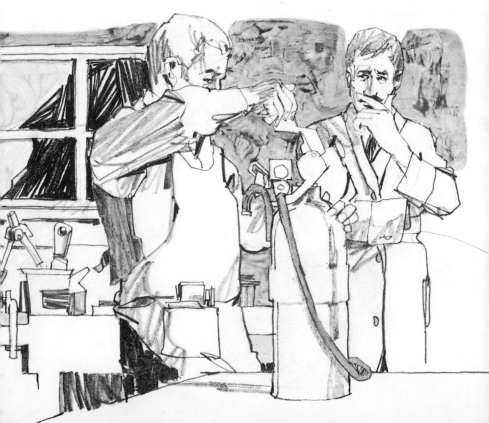

When the new invention was ready to be tested, they drove to the bank of the Marne River outside the city. It was January, and very cold.

Cousteau waded into the river, the aqualung strapped to his

back. He slipped its mouthpiece between his lips and plunged into the dirty water.

On shore, Gagnan watched air bubbles burst as they came to the surface. Suddenly they stopped. He was about to dive into the river, when Cousteau popped to the surface.

"Jacques, I thought you drowned," he cried.

Shivering, Cousteau crawled up onto the bank.

"I was standing on my head," he said. "The air supply almost stopped. I couldn't breathe."

Back in the laboratory, they rebuilt the aqualung.

Summer came, and the aqualung was ready for its first test in the ocean.

With face mask, fins, and aqualung in place, Cousteau swam out to sea and dove. He breathed through the mouthpiece. Air came in a sweet even flow. He breathed out, and a stream of silver bubbles danced away toward the shimmering surface above.

The aqualung worked.

We are free at last, he thought, *to swim across miles of country no man has known ... with our flesh feeling what the fish scales know.*

Almost three-quarters of the earth's surface is water. The aqualung would aid in its exploration.

That summer Cousteau and
two friends, Philippe Tailliez and
Frédéric Dumas, made five hun-
dred dives with the aqualung.
Deep in the sea they found
sunken ships.

After building a watertight case
for his camera, Cousteau made
the first movie of aqualung divers
swimming like fish around sea-
weed-covered wrecks.

Enemy soldiers patrolling the beaches ignored Cousteau and his strange-looking equipment. "They considered me a harmless nut," he said.

He wanted to be ignored. He was now leading a secret life, working for the French underground.

"After the war is over," he told his friends, "I'm going to have a special research ship where divers and oceanographers can work together."

But the war was not over yet. Bombs lay hidden under waves in French harbors. Cousteau knew what he must do.

He went to an old naval base and put up a sign that read

UNDERSEA RESEARCH GROUP

HELP WANTED

Sailors joined, and learned to dive with the aqualung. Soon they were at work in the harbors diving for bombs and taking them away.

After the war, Cousteau saw an old minesweeper, *Calypso.* He knew he had found his ship. He bought *Calypso* and went to work turning it into a research ship.

White paint soon covered *Ca-lypso*'s sides. On the deck an anti-shark cage hung from the new crane. If sharks appeared, the cage would be lowered over the side and divers could swim inside for safety.

Special cameras and floodlights for taking pictures underwater were stored in the ship's new photo laboratory. Fish tanks and test tubes filled a small science laboratory nearby.

Taking leave from the Navy, Captain Cousteau set out with a crew of scientists, photographers, and divers to learn about the sea.

On one voyage, they found a Greek ship that had been buried under the sea for 2,200 years.

On another voyage, Cousteau dove deep into the sea where darkness makes bright colors look grey. Using special underwater lights, he took the first color pictures of the red and yellow coral that live there.

In the winter of 1955, *Calypso* made a trip to the eastern coast of Africa looking for a place to finish filming an underwater movie.

Off Assumption Island, it dropped anchor in a clear-blue bay.

Cousteau pulled on his face mask, climbed down the diving ladder, and slipped into the water.

Gliding down, he passed through a cloud of speckled fish swimming under the belly of the ship.

A butterfly fish sprang from a crack in the coral. It darted in front of Cousteau's mask and peered at the face inside.

Cousteau blinked in surprise.

Fish had fled from him and his divers on other expeditions. Why didn't these fish fear men?

Suddenly Cousteau knew the answer. He swam up to the diving ladder, where the crew had gathered.

"We have found a wilderness where man is unknown," he said. "These fish have never seen a hook or a hunter.

"No one is to take a spear gun below. We have a chance for a great experiment . . . a chance for a peaceful invasion of the sea to see if we can be accepted among the fish and live in their world."

The divers took bags of chopped meat from the ship's galley and slid into the water. When they opened the bags, fish snatched the floating food.

One great brown fish ate from
a diver's hand. The diver patted
his spotted head and scratched
his belly. The men named him
Ulysses.

One day Ulysses snatched the bag of meat from a diver and swallowed it whole.

For days afterward he lay on his side on the sandy bottom.

Cousteau and his divers went
on with their work. They used
the meat bag to coax small fish in
front of the camera.

Suddenly Ulysses appeared.

He raced in front of the camera, knocked over the flood-light with his tail, and chased away the smaller fish.

The anti-shark cage was lowered and its door was opened. Ulysses swam in and the door was shut. He was in jail. When the last picture had been taken, and Cousteau and his men were ready to leave, Ulysses was freed.

For a while Cousteau and his men had lived in the world of fish.

Cousteau's movie was called *The Silent World.* In the United States it won an Academy Award. In France it won a Grand Prize at the Cannes Film Festival.

From the movie screen, Ulysses peered out at audiences in many lands. He was a star.

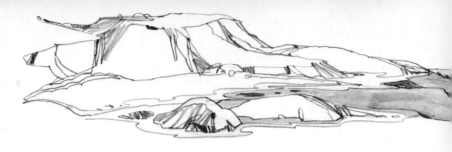

Cousteau was busier than ever. In Monaco he became director of one of the world's largest marine museums and laboratories. Scientists from all over the world went there to study.

He began to think of the future.

Around many countries a shelf of land stretches out for miles under the sea before sloping down to the ocean floor thousands and thousands of feet below. *Someday men will live in undersea cities built on this continental shelf*, Cousteau thought.

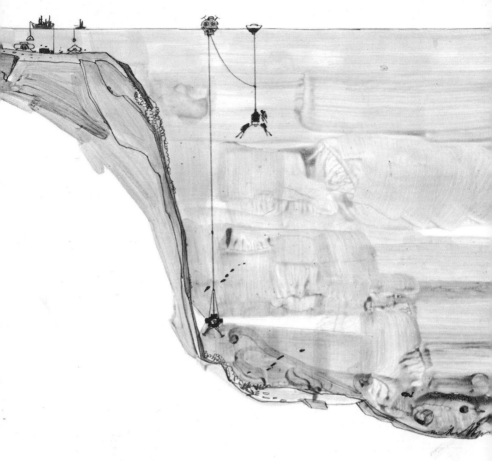

They will search for oil and
minerals there and cultivate undersea fish farms. From shelf
stations they will travel down to
explore and film the ocean floor.

45

But the aqualung could take divers down only about 250 feet. New equipment would be needed to take them deeper. Cousteau built a diving saucer. Like an octopus, it moved through the sea by shooting out jets of water.

In the summer of 1963 Cousteau set out to prove that people could live and work in the sea.

He and his crew built the first undersea human colony on a shelf 35 feet beneath the Red Sea. Five divers, oceanauts, lived there for one month in a starfish-shaped house where air pressure kept the water from coming in.

Swimming in and out of the
house through an open hatch in
the floor, the oceanauts collected
fish and algae to study in their

laboratory. Returning from field
trips at night, they ate and went
to bed in their home beneath the
waves.

Near the house stood an under-sea garage for Cousteau's diving saucer. It, too, was air-filled.

One morning Cousteau and a diver took the saucer downward to the sea floor. The water outside grew dark.

The saucer landed gently on the sandy bottom, 1,000 feet below the surface. Cousteau switched on a floodlight. The saucer prowled along the gloomy bottom.

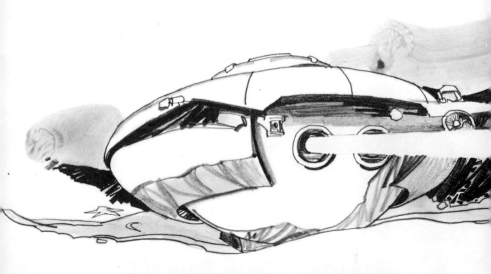

Surprised by the light, a band of squid pivoted on their heads in the sand. They held their tentacles over their heads like umbrellas.

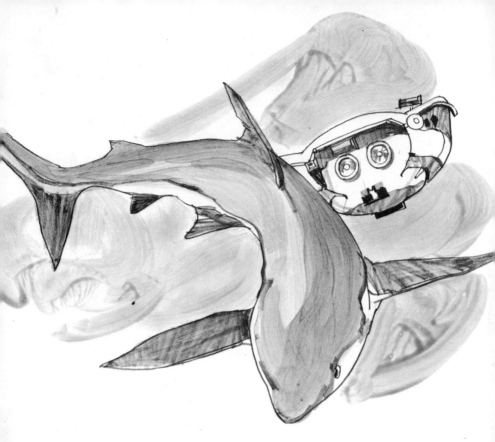

Transparent fish swam above the saucer. Through their glass-like bodies Cousteau could see their red and black organs.

Suddenly a huge bull shark— 22 feet from head to fin—came into view.

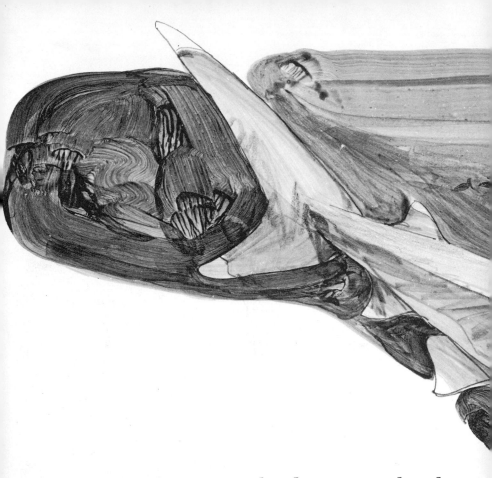

His gleaming body wove back
and forth through the light. The
saucer's camera clicked away.

The shark turned and swam
off. The powerful sweep of his
tail rocked the saucer.

Back inside the garage, Cousteau climbed out of the saucer and smiled. His diving saucer was the first undersea vessel to travel to and from its own undersea base.

After leaving the Red Sea, Cousteau set out on the longest expedition of his life. Aboard *Calypso*, he would spend years wandering and exploring the earth's waterways.

As he traveled around the world, Cousteau made films and wrote books that won many honors.

With him, as on many trips, were Madame Cousteau and their son Philippe. Their older son, Jean-Michel, also loved the sea. On land, he worked as an architect.

In the Atlantic Philippe recorded the song of the singing humpback whale. Near the Arctic

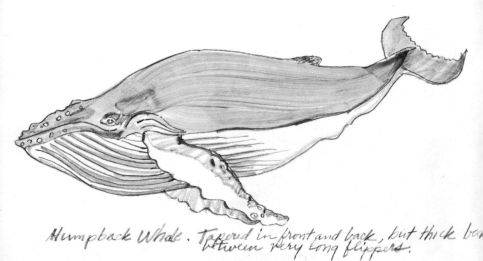

Humpback Whale. Tapered in front and back, but thick between very long flippers.

Cousteau filmed walrus riding
through the sea on floating ice-
bergs. Off the coast of Mexico he
searched for sharks asleep in
caves. In the Aegean Sea he
hunted for the legendary city of
Atlantis.

Cousteau now traveled back to seas he had explored years before. What he saw made him sad and angry.

Water, once clear, was now clouded. Now only a few fish swam where large schools swirled before.

Chemicals and sewage from the land poisoned the seas. Oil and garbage from tankers and other ships floated on the surface.

"The oceans are dying," he said. He wanted to try to save the seas, which were being destroyed by man.

In books, films, and lectures, he has shown people that the sea and its creatures are fragile.

"If civilization is going to invade the waters of the earth," he said, "then let it be, first of all, to carry a message of respect—respect for all life."

Many are taking up his work.

Like Jacques-Yves Cousteau, they know that man must save the sea if he is to save himself.

The Author

GENIE IVERSON, a native of California and a lover of marine biology, was graduated from the University of California at Berkeley with a major in English literature and a minor in journalism.

Before turning her talents to the writing of history and biography for children she was a newspaper reporter and feature writer. When she is not writing she enjoys both photography and tennis.

The Artist

HAL ASHMEAD studied at Cornell College in Iowa, The American Academy of Art in Chicago, and the Art Center School in Los Angeles.

A member of the Society of Illustrators, he has illustrated for many national publications, including the *New York Times, Cosmopolitan, Children's Digest,* Scholastic Magazines, and *Mankind.*

Mr. Ashmead was also the sketch artist covering the Sirhan-Sirhan trial for CBS.